THE THRIVING WORKPLACE SERIES

VOLUME 1

NEXT-LEVEL TEAMWORK

The 5 Tensions to Manage for High-Performance Teams

TIM ARNOLD

Leaders for Leaders Inc.
2866 Prince William Street
PO Box 25
Jordan Station, ON, L0R 1S0
(289) 723 2546

Ordering Information:
Special discounts are available on quantity purchases by corporations, associations, and others. For details, contact the publisher at the address or phone number above.

www.LeadersForLeaders.ca

Printed in Canada

CONTENTS

THE THRIVING WORKPLACE SERIES

You want to be a great leader. Someone who makes a positive difference through the work you do *and* in the lives of the people you do it with. A person who inspires others through your positivity and passion. The kind of leader everyone wants to work for.

In order to do this, you need to be successful at three things:

1. Building effective teams,

2. Leading people through change, and

3. Fostering a healthy workplace culture.

The problem is most organizations are broken, which forces you to spend too much of your time wrestling with conflicting values and refereeing unhealthy friction. This can leave you feeling discouraged and unsupported.

It shouldn't be this hard! You deserve a trusted roadmap to help you build the thriving workplace you know is possible. The Thriving Workplace Series is that roadmap.

Through my experience owning a for-profit business, launching a social enterprise, and directing a homeless shelter, I understand how hard it is to lead in challenging situations. This is why I'm driven to help leaders just like you navigate the road to success.

In working with incredible leaders ranging from Nobel Peace Prize winners to Fortune 500 CEOs, I've learned that the secret to success is to embrace the very thing most people avoid: tension. Great leaders find healthy tension in the following key areas:

Building Effective Teams
(Volume 1 of The Thriving Workplace Series)

1. Focusing on Tasks AND Relationships

2. Leveraging Structure AND Flexibility

3. Communicating Truthfully AND Tactfully

4. Promoting Collaboration AND Independence

5. Increasing Empowerment AND Accountability

Leading Change
(Volume 2 of The Thriving Workplace Series)

1. Embracing Innovation AND Preserving Consistency

2. Validating Facts AND Feelings

3. Focusing on the Short Term AND the Long Term

4. Promoting Planning AND Execution

5. Valuing Complexity AND Simplicity

Developing a Healthy Culture
(Volume 3 of The Thriving Workplace Series)

1. Focusing on People AND Results

2. Respecting Rules AND Risk

3. Fostering Critical Analysis AND Encouragement

4. Promoting Decentralized Freedom AND Centralized Coordination

5. Valuing Work AND Home

Too many people spend most of their waking hours working for unhealthy organizations and in dysfunctional teams. Sadly, one of the main reasons for this is ineffective leaders who don't have the skills or courage to face tension head-on. But not you!

The purpose of this playbook series is to help you tap into the power of healthy tension so that you can unleash your true leadership potential and help your organization thrive.

By putting the concepts and principles of these playbooks into action, you will make your leadership stand out from the crowd. You will be responsible for creating an environment where everyone loves their work, who they get to do it with, and the impact it's having.

Let's do this!

NEXT-LEVEL TEAMWORK
The 5 Crux Tensions

1. Focusing on Tasks AND Relationships
2. Leveraging Structure AND Flexibility
3. Communicating Truthfully AND Tactfully
4. Promoting Collaboration AND Independence
5. Increasing Empowerment AND Accountability

To thank you for purchasing this playbook, I want to provide you with a free resource that will allow you to create a personal action plan around key concepts and big ideas.

Simply visit www.timarnold.ca/teams to download the Personal Action Plan. This digital journal includes chapter summaries, tension maps, and assessment grids as well as space for you to create a plan you can immediately put into action.

WWW.TIMARNOLD.CA/TEAMS

CHAPTER 1

MOST TEAMS DON'T WORK!

Why Most People Settle for Dysfunction
(and How to Overcome It)

I 'd like to introduce you to Priya and Matt. On many levels, these two individuals are very similar. Both are committed to their family and friends. Both are hardworking and conscientious. And as professionals, they both want to work in a team that's fully engaged. They want the kind of culture where team members love working together.

But there is one huge difference between them. Every Sunday evening, Priya gets excited about the week ahead. She looks forward to reconnecting with her team and tackling the challenges and opportunities before her. Matt, on the other hand, gets a feeling of dread when he thinks about Monday mornings. He is shamefully reminded of how unenthused he is about his job and the company he works for, not to mention the divisive team relationships that stress him out.

How can the Sunday evenings of two similar people be so incredibly different?

Priya and Matt are both skilled at their jobs and enjoy the profession they are in. And they both work for respected organizations. But while Priya can't imagine working anywhere else and is a valuable contributor to the company, Matt stops at just getting his job done; he never goes above and beyond. His energy is much more focused on scrolling job boards and daydreaming about better options.

Here's the sad news: There are a lot more Matts than there are Priyas in today's workplace. Studies suggest that 75% of teams in leading corporations are dysfunctional.[1] And because close to seven in 10 workers have had negative team experiences, only 24% of professionals would choose to work in teams if they were given the option.[2]

The reality is most teams don't work!

As someone who works with professionals like Priya and Matt every week, I understand how discouraging and frustrating it can be to spend most of your time working in a dysfunctional team. But there's hope! For the past 20 years, I've helped hundreds of teams across the world—from United Nations weapons inspectors and C-suites of Fortune 500 companies to the front line of small not-for-profits—move beyond dysfunction and mediocrity and into alignment and high performance.

And here's what it takes:

For your team to work, you must learn to embrace the very thing that most teams avoid—tension! In order to experience next-level teamwork, you must learn to manage the following five tensions in a healthy way:

1. Focusing on Tasks AND Relationships

2. Leveraging Structure AND Flexibility

3. Communicating Truthfully AND Tactfully

4. Promoting Collaboration AND Independence

5. Increasing Empowerment AND Accountability

Let me explain. There are two types of challenges your team deals with each day:

1. **Problems to Solve** – These are challenges for which there is one right or superior answer, and all you need to do is pick that option and move on. They require Either/Or thinking. For example, should we choose Salesforce or HubSpot? Which social media platforms should we focus on? What sessions should we include at the company off-site?

2. **Tensions to Manage** – These are ongoing challenges for which, instead of choosing one option, you need to find healthy tension between conflicting values. They require Both/And thinking. For example, how do we embrace change and preserve stability? What does it look like to be optimistic and realistic? As a leader, how do I care for others and care for myself?

If you're dealing with a tension to manage but you treat it like a problem to solve, you're in trouble.

Think of breathing. You manage the tension between inhaling and exhaling about 22,000 times a day. You can't wake up and say, "I think it's an inhale day today." Inhaling and exhaling are a package deal. You can't survive with just one and not the other. And so long as you manage this tension well, you'll stay healthy and strong. If you don't manage this tension well, however, you'll become blue in the face.

The same phenomenon exists at work. If you treat any of the five team tensions as if they are problems to solve, your team is destined for dysfunction. However, if you learn to manage these tensions well, you will tap into next-level teamwork.

LET'S FIGHT OFF TEAM DYSFUNCTION TOGETHER

Like Matt, you deserve better than wasting your time and talent in a dysfunctional, disengaged team. When you learn how to tap into the power of healthy tension like Priya, you gain the ability to unleash the individual and collaborative potential of your team and help the organization thrive.

By working through the chapters of this short playbook, you will gain the ability to understand, assess, and leverage each of the five tensions.

Let's get started.

A SPECIAL NOTE FOR PEOPLE LEADERS

When it comes to high-performance teamwork, every member of the team has a role to play. However, if you're a supervisor or manager, you have a heightened privilege and responsibility to put the ideas of this playbook into practice.

As a people leader, you have the chance to guide people toward a common vision and be a catalyst for great work. You also have the opportunity to motivate, develop, and inspire the people that report to you so they can become better versions of themselves.

At the same time, there is a huge responsibility in being a supervisor or manager. You are now the biggest factor in determining whether your staff's team experience is a positive one or a negative one. You will control whether it's safe or unsafe to embrace these five tensions. Your behaviours will make it clear to others whether relationships and collaboration truly matter.

As Uncle Ben wisely said to a young Peter Parker, "with great power comes great responsibility." Remember, the strength of the leader equals the strength of the team.

CHAPTER 2

BUILDING TEAM TRUST

Focusing on Tasks AND Relationships

TASK FOCUSED — *Skillfully managing time and people to meet deadlines and accomplish goals. Moving things forward, getting work done, and checking things off your list.*

RELATIONSHIP FOCUSED — *Deliberately investing in the satisfaction, well-being, and connection of team members. Developing an understanding and appreciation for one another as co-workers and as people.*

STEP 1: UNDERSTAND

Finding a way to deliberately focus on *both* tasks *and* relationships is a make-it-or-break-it leadership skill if you want to experience next-level teamwork.

As the following graphic illustrates, there are positive results that come exclusively from focusing on both. At the same time, there are inevitable negative results if you overfocus on one side to the neglect of the other.

TENSION
Focusing on Tasks AND Relationships

POSITIVE RESULTS OF FOCUSING ON TASKS

- Ability to focus and get things done
- Deadlines are met
- People feel a sense of accomplishment

POSITIVE RESULTS OF FOCUSING ON RELATIONSHIPS

- Builds trust and belonging within the team
- People learn and leverage each others' strengths
- Work is more enjoyable and fun

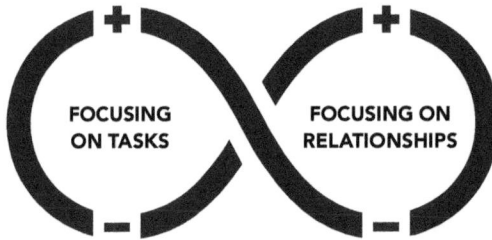

FOCUSING ON TASKS **FOCUSING ON RELATIONSHIPS**

NEGATIVE RESULTS WHEN OVERDONE

- People feel isolated and unsupported
- Minimizes collaboration and trust
- People blame one another when things go wrong

NEGATIVE RESULTS WHEN OVERDONE

- People have a hard time getting their work done
- Deadlines are missed
- People are frustrated by distractions and drama

Based on the Polarity Map® and Principles of Barry Johnson and Polarity Partnerships LLC

STEP 2: ASSESS

Reflect on this past season. Has your team had the time and freedom to be task focused? Have you also been deliberate about building effective relationships with one another?

Take a look at the following chart and assess in which of the four quadrants your team is currently spending the most time.

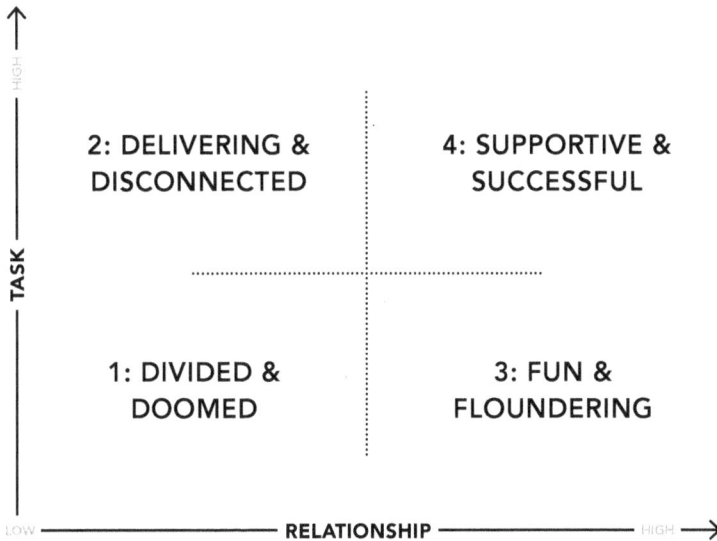

STEP 3: LEVERAGE

Regardless of which quadrant you are currently in, the goal is to spend more time in quadrant four. The good news is that there are practical things you can do to get there. It is possible to experience the positive results of being *both* task *and* relationship focused, ultimately helping your team to be more supportive and successful.

FOCUSING ON RELATIONSHIPS

"We must establish a personal connection with each other.
Connection before content. Without relatedness, no work can occur."

– PETER BLOCK

FOUNDER OF THE COMMON GOOD COLLECTIVE

Connection before content! This is a great motto for your team to live by. When you prioritize connection, you will build trust, maximize collaboration, and make work more enjoyable.

Here are some simple and actionable things you can do daily, weekly, and quarterly to gain or maintain a healthy focus on relationships.

Daily – Plato wisely said, "You can discover more about a person in an hour of play than in a year of conversation." In other words, being relationship focused doesn't have to take a ton of time. Whenever you have a meeting scheduled, deliberately start with 5 to 10 minutes of relational connection before getting down to work.

This can be as simple as having each person answer a question of the day. For example:

- Outside of work, what are you excited about in the month ahead?

- What are you learning these days?

- What was your first job or worst job?

- If you could experience any TV show as your real life, which show would you choose?

- What album, song, or podcast are you listening to these days?

You'll find that when you carve out five to 10 minutes to focus on building relationships, the rest of the meeting will end up being much more engaging and productive.

Weekly – Create space to celebrate wins. This can be added to an existing meeting, or it can become a new 15-minute Monday-morning ritual. During this time, have team members share things that they're proud of from the previous week or give a shout-out to coworkers for their great work and/or accomplishments. This creates a culture of celebration and recognition.

Quarterly – Each season, dedicate at least a half-day to get the team out of the office, or if you have a remote team, get people in a room face-to-face. Before getting together, determine your purpose for gathering. Whether your team simply needs to have some fun together, do some in-person learning, or a combination of both, ensure you plan your activities accordingly.

Ideas for an off-site focused on fun connections:

- Enjoy a meal together.

- Tackle an escape room.

- Serve lunch at a local homeless shelter.

Ideas for a gathering focused on learning:

- Organize an expert to lead a professional development session in an area of growth for your team.

- Learn about one another's strengths and weaknesses through a personality assessment (e.g., Myers-Briggs, Working Genius, etc.).

- Collaboratively develop your work plan for the season ahead to maximize alignment and buy-in.

FOCUSING ON TASKS

"Focus on being productive instead of busy."

– TIM FERRISS

AUTHOR OF THE 4-HOUR WORKWEEK

Just because team members claim to be busy doesn't necessarily mean that the team is being productive. Experiencing the true upsides of being task focused means that deadlines are met, team members are engaged, and there's a sense of accomplishment among the group.

In order to get the full benefits of being task focused, all team members must be able to answer yes to each of these three questions:

1. **Am I clear on what my piece is, and do I have the time and resources to deliver on it?**

The research is clear[1] that, in order to stay engaged, team members need to fully understand what is expected of them. They need to know what unique piece they bring to the puzzle. And simply having a job description is not good enough.

Team members need to know what delivering on these expectations looks like each day, week, and season. They also must have the basic resources required to deliver on these expectations. This means that they have the time, training, equipment, and teamwork necessary for success.

2. **Are my fellow team members engaged and committed to owning their pieces?**

Ownership and engagement are contagious. One of the biggest factors in keeping individuals task focused is ensuring they are surrounded by other team members who are also task focused.[2] And as you might guess, one of the fastest ways to see team engagement decline is when team members don't hold each other accountable when they fail to deliver on expectations.

3. **Can I constantly assess whether we are winning or losing?**

There's something within us—individually and collectively—that wants to win. And tapping into the upside of healthy competition is a great way to keep the team task focused. That's why it's so important to have metrics that team members can check at any given time to assess their success or failure. This can be in the form of a simple team dashboard with metrics, graphics, and/or KPIs that all team members can understand.

BUILDING TEAM TRUST

I've been working in the team-building and leadership-development industry for decades now, and one thing that has been consistently clear throughout the years is that team effectiveness rises and falls based on the level of trust. Not only is this supported by countless studies and books,[3] but I've also seen it lived out in my experience working with teams across the world.

In his book, *The 7 Habits of Highly Effective People*,[4] author Stephen Covey describes trust as a bank account. He says that every interaction between team members is either a deposit or a withdrawal, causing the trust account to go up or down.

For example, deposits to the trust account are made when team members get to know one another beyond their job description and have a genuine appreciation and respect for one another as people. Deposits are also made every time team members own their pieces and deliver on one another's expectations.

Finding a healthy tension between *both* tasks *and* relationships is the fastest and most effective way to build team trust and take teamwork to the next level.

CHAPTER 3

SET UP FOR SUCCESS

Leveraging Structure AND Flexibility

STRUCTURE — *A clear, systematic framework for when and how things are done. This incorporates product and service delivery as well as team expectations and interactions.*

FLEXIBILITY — *The ability to bend, adapt, and modify. Adjusting how things are done based on unique strengths, individual needs, and specific situations.*

STEP 1: UNDERSTAND

F inding the right blend between structure and flexibility is critical to experiencing next-level teamwork.

As the following graphic illustrates, there are positive results that come exclusively from focusing on both. At the same time, there are inevitable negative results if you overfocus on one side to the neglect of the other.

TENSION
Leveraging Structure AND Flexibility

POSITIVE RESULTS OF
LEVERAGING STRUCTURE

- Expectations are fair and consistent
- Focuses time and resources
- Solidifies proven practices

POSITIVE RESULTS OF
LEVERAGING FLEXIBILITY

- Capitalizes on people's unique strengths
- Creates a culture of understanding and equity
- Allows individuals and teams to be responsive

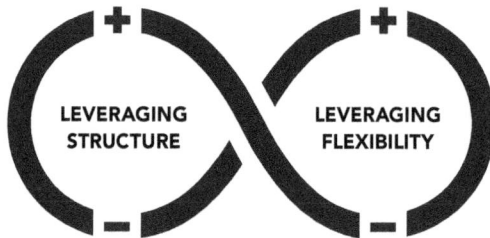

LEVERAGING STRUCTURE — **LEVERAGING FLEXIBILITY**

NEGATIVE RESULTS
WHEN **OVERDONE**

- People feel stifled
- Creates a culture of all work, no play
- Misses out on opportunities and new approaches

NEGATIVE RESULTS
WHEN **OVERDONE**

- People become distracted and misaligned
- Lack of equality leads to resentment
- Creates chaos and confusion

STEP 2: ASSESS

Reflect on this past season. Has your team experienced all the benefits that come from having a high level of structure? Have you also been adaptable enough to tap into the benefits that come from a high level of flexibility?

Take a look at the following chart and assess in which of the four quadrants your team is currently spending the most time.

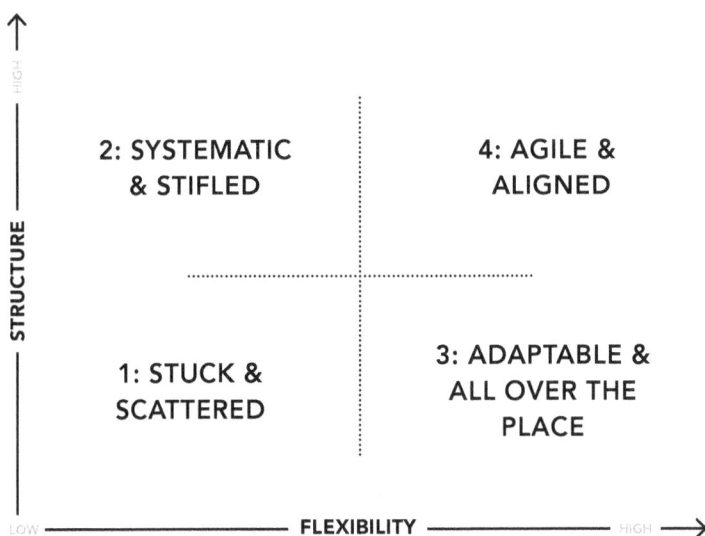

STEP 3: LEVERAGE

Regardless of which quadrant you currently find yourself in, the goal is to spend more time in quadrant four. The good news is that there are practical things you can do to get there. It is possible to experience the positive results of *both* structure *and* flexibility so you can become more agile and aligned.

LEVERAGING STRUCTURE

1. Clarify Expectations

In the months leading up to Becky's and my wedding day, we participated in a series of marriage mentoring sessions. One thing our mentors taught us, which turned out to be incredibly wise and helpful, was to be prepared for the fact that both of us were going into the marriage with a long list of expectations for the other person. The problem was, we wouldn't know what those expectations were until they were violated. Our mentors stressed how important it was to talk about an expectation in order to get clarity around it moving forward.

This is true at work as well. Everyone comes to the team with different assumptions about what is expected (or not expected) of them in these four areas:

- **Punctuality**
  - » Is it OK to arrive to work 10 minutes late if I make up the time at the end of the day?

- **Communication**
  - » When should I CC all team members on an email and when is that annoying?

- **Meeting Behaviours**
  - » Is it OK to keep my camera off during a virtual meeting or discretely respond to a text during an in-person meeting?

- **Availability**
  - » Is it OK to call or text a colleague about a work question after hours?

When it comes to all four of these areas, it's important for leaders to be clear on what expectations are part of how the team is structured. And going back to the advice of my marriage mentors, it's also important to pay attention when a team member fails to meet an expectation. Rather than getting frustrated or annoyed, use the situation as a learning opportunity to help them understand why the structure exists and the benefit it provides.

2. It's good for you!

As a parent, there are certain structures and expectations I have that I know my kids will dislike, yet I enforce them because I know what's good for them. Whether it's eating their vegetables, doing weekly chores around the house, or getting to bed on time, I know they'd choose not to do these things if they were given the option. But they're not given the option because I know these boundaries will serve them well, and at the end of the day—I'm responsible.

Similarly, at work, there are specific structures and expectations you need to put in place that your team members probably wouldn't choose if they were given the option. These are things like attending meetings, keeping client information up-to-date in your CRM, or at times, going to the office to work face-to-face with other team members. But you know that these things are the best way for you to serve your clients and for the team to work effectively. Certain things are not optional. Leadership means being responsible, which sometimes means expecting people to go beyond doing what they want and instead do what is best.

LEVERAGING FLEXIBILITY

"Average managers play checkers, while great managers play chess."

– MARCUS BUCKINGHAM

CO-CREATOR OF STRENGTHSFINDER

1. Make the Most of Strengths

In a *Harvard Business Review* article, "What Great Managers Do,"[1] author Marcus Buckingham shares the results from a study of 80,000 managers. The research demonstrates how the most effective leaders with the highest-performing teams were deliberate in taking a flexible approach to managing each team member. They viewed their team as a game of chess as opposed to a game of checkers.

In checkers, all the pieces move in the same way. In chess, each piece moves in a different way, and great chess players uniquely leverage each piece. Similarly, great leaders know the strengths, weaknesses, and individuality of each employee, and they have the flexibility required to unleash each person's greatest contribution.

Practically speaking, taking a chess approach means team members have options around working more collaboratively or independently depending on their skill set and personality. It also means training and development can be customized depending on people's individual learning styles. By paying attention to what strengths and what weaknesses people have, leaders can revise job descriptions over time to allow team members to do more of the work they're great at.

2. Equity vs. Equality

Equality means that people are given the same things and are held to the same expectations. In teams, having certain structures in place that promote equality is important to maintain consistency and minimize resentment and favouritism. However, true fairness does not always mean that everyone gets the same thing; it means that everyone gets what they need. It goes beyond equality and embraces equity. Think of equality as giving everyone the same pair of shoes, while equity is giving everyone a pair of shoes that fit.

Your team needs the flexibility to embrace equity, ensuring that everyone gets what they need to deliver on expectations and thrive in their job. This requires the relational investment I discussed in the previous chapter in order to produce empathy. As team members truly understand one another's unique story, they grow in their level of grace and are more open to accommodating people's individual needs.

As a leader, embracing equity requires courage. Having everyone get the same thing is much easier than ensuring everyone gets what they need. It's trickier and more controversial to provide personalized accommodations, allow variable time away from work, and modify project expectations, but it's worth it! With more and more evidence pointing to the need for psychological safety in teams,[2] taking an equitable approach where people feel that their individual needs are understood and met is a core foundation for this type of high-performance environment.

SET UP FOR SUCCESS

As I'm writing this chapter, the world is still coming out of the COVID-19 pandemic, and not a day goes by where I'm not hearing examples of *unhealthy* tension between structure and flexibility, specifically when it comes to remote versus in-person team strategies. After experiencing the downsides of overdone flexibility, some leaders are now taking the approach of forcing their teams back to the office with a 100% return to "the way it was." And without fail, they're shocked and frustrated by the amount of resistance and resentment they're facing from their teams.

Other leaders are simply (and naively) accepting the fact that remote work and Zoom-based relationships are the new reality and are putting no structures in place that require people to connect and work in person. Sadly, they're finding alignment, collaboration, and morale beginning to tank within their teams.

The leaders who are tapping into an amazing competitive advantage right now are the ones who refuse to take an Either/Or approach and instead embrace *both* structure *and* flexibility in their back-to-work attitude. They know that having certain structures and expectations around working together, whether in person or remotely, will result in increased collaboration and team morale.

They are also leveraging many of the amazing strategies and technologies businesses acquired during the pandemic that allow teams to effectively collaborate in a remote and flexible way. And as a result, their teams are more productive and positive than ever. They've realized that leveraging structure AND flexibility is the best way to set their teams up for success and experience next-level teamwork.

CHAPTER 4

COURAGEOUS CONVERSATIONS

Communicating Truthfully AND Tactfully

TRUTHFULLY — *Sharing what you are feeling and thinking in a clear and accurate way. Being open and honest even in difficult or uncomfortable situations.*

TACTFULLY — *Being mindful of the impact of your words and skilled at communicating in a way that is kind and diplomatic. Focused on being understood over being heard.*

STEP 1: UNDERSTAND

Next-level teamwork requires exceptional communication skills. To make this happen, team members need to be *both* truthful *and* tactful with one another.

As the following graphic illustrates, there are positive results that come exclusively from focusing on both. At the same time, there are inevitable negative results if you overfocus on one side to the neglect of the other.

TENSION
Communicating Truthfully AND Tactfully

POSITIVE RESULTS OF
COMMUNICATING TRUTHFULLY

- Communication is clear and direct
- Team members speak up for what they believe in
- Allows for healthy debate

POSITIVE RESULTS OF
COMMUNICATING TACTFULLY

- Communication is kind and empathetic
- People feel less defensive and listen more attentively
- Creates a respectful and safe culture

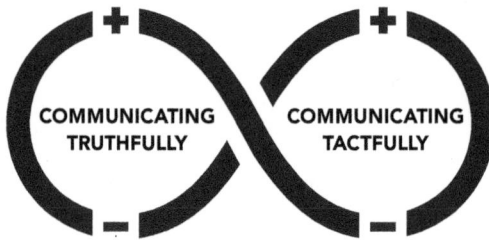

COMMUNICATING TRUTHFULLY   **COMMUNICATING TACTFULLY**

NEGATIVE RESULTS
WHEN OVERDONE

- Causes unnecessary hurt and conflict
- People shut down and don't hear the message
- Creates a defensive and argumentative culture

NEGATIVE RESULTS
WHEN OVERDONE

- Communication is vague and confusing
- Team members hold back, which limits their impact
- People don't hear what they need to hear

STEP 2: ASSESS

Reflect on your meetings and interactions this past season. Has your team experienced all the benefits that come from communicating truthfully? Have you also been tapping into the benefits that come from communicating tactfully?

Take a look at the following chart and assess in which of the four quadrants your team is currently spending the most time.

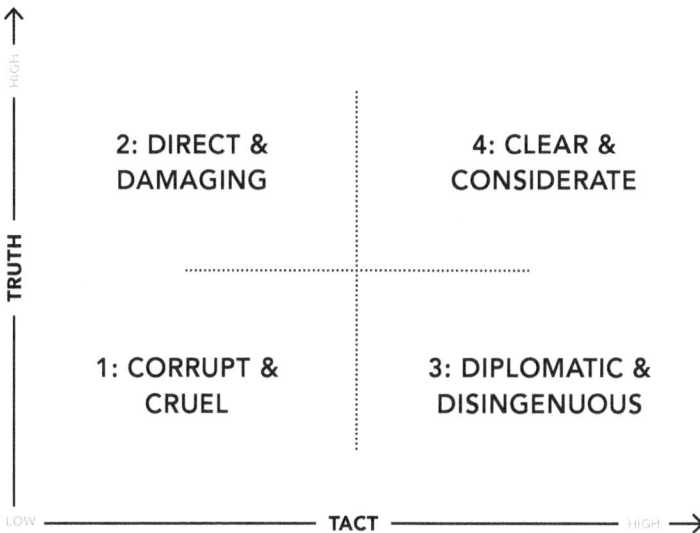

	HIGH	
2: DIRECT & DAMAGING		**4: CLEAR & CONSIDERATE**
1: CORRUPT & CRUEL		**3: DIPLOMATIC & DISINGENUOUS**

TRUTH ↑ HIGH

LOW ——————— TACT ——————— HIGH →

STEP 3: LEVERAGE

Regardless of which quadrant you currently find yourself in, the goal is to spend more time in quadrant four. The good news is that there are practical things you can do to gain the positive results of *both* truth *and* tact so that communication in your team is clear and considerate.

PASSIVE, AGGRESSIVE, OR ASSERTIVE?

As a communicator, if you overfocus on tact to the neglect of truth, you can easily become passive. Here are some signs that you may be a passive communicator:

- You feel anxious when talking about yourself and sharing your thoughts, feelings, and perspectives.

- You bottle things up to avoid uncomfortable situations.

- You miss out on opportunities and others miss out on your full contribution because you worry too much about hurting others' feelings.

On the other hand, if you overfocus on truth to the neglect of tact, you can easily become aggressive. Here are some signs that you may be an aggressive communicator:

- You have little interest in other people's perspectives, needs, or feelings.

- You can be forceful in promoting your views, sometimes using manipulation or intimidation.

- You're often one-sided in your approach, leaving little room for compromise (i.e., yes or no; agree or disagree).

The goal is not to swing from being passive to aggressive or vice versa. At the same time, you want to avoid becoming an unhealthy mix of both, which is referred to as passive-aggressive. The goal is to become assertive.

Assertiveness is a beautiful blend of focusing on your own needs, values, and point of view *and* focusing on the needs, values, and points of view of other people. You're able to say what needs to be said, and you express it in a way this is easy to understand.

To become assertive, you need to fully embrace *both* truthful *and* tactful communication.

FROM PASSIVE TO ASSERTIVE

Count the Costs – If you are a passive communicator—someone who overfocuses on tact to the neglect of truth—you will naturally weigh the costs of speaking up or having an uncomfortable conversation:

- People may not agree with you.

- You may end up looking foolish.

- Other people may get upset with you.

However, you often forget to weigh the costs of not having the conversation:

- You're not being true to yourself.

- You're not bringing your full contribution and expertise to the project you're working on.

- You're failing to provide others with development opportunities.

It's important to take time to consider the cost of holding back so that you gain the confidence needed to speak your truth when it's required.

Keep Breathing – If you're someone who defaults to tact over truth, and you're trying to become more assertive, you need to anticipate that it will be uncomfortable. The emotional part of your brain will often become triggered, overpowering the logical and rational parts. This can result in feelings of stress and anxiety, and your heart can feel like it's pounding out of your chest.

Be prepared for this and try to stay focused on your breathing. Studies have found that in times of stress, deliberately taking good, deep breaths for as little as 18 seconds (7 seconds breathing in and 11 seconds breathing out) can lower blood pressure, slow the heart rate, and minimize feeling "emotionally hijacked."[1] Remember the wise words of Dr. Susan David who reminds us that "discomfort is the price of admission to a meaningful life."[2]

FROM AGGRESSIVE TO ASSERTIVE

Practice Restraint – If you are an aggressive communicator—someone who overfocuses on truth to the neglect of tact—you'll find it easy to dominate conversations and minimize the insight and impact of other people. One simple trick that will still allow you to speak up and contribute but in a much more assertive way is to discipline yourself not to be the first or last person to speak in a meeting or conversation. Even if you have lots of ideas or concerns, do your best to hear from others first.

If no one is speaking up, you could start by letting the group know that you have thoughts to share, but you're eager to hear from others first. And if you notice that you're the one talking as the discussion comes to a close, you might want to ask for the group's input by inquiring about their current thoughts and feelings.

Ask Better Questions – When you're communicating in an aggressive way, you will often take an Either/Or perspective, and as a result, you will ask questions that can be answered with a simple yes or no:

- Do you agree or disagree?

- Did you like working with that team?

- Did you enjoy the meeting?

- Are you on board with the decision?

- Shouldn't the meeting be in-person?

Unfortunately, this binary approach to communication leaves little room for dialogue and creativity. Instead, push yourself to reframe your closed questions into open-ended, probing questions:

- What are your thoughts on the situation?

- How do you think we can improve this process?

- Can you tell me more about what you mean by that?

- What are ways we could better collaborate in the next month?

- What else would you like to add to this conversation?

COURAGEOUS CONVERSATIONS

I was raised in a loving and supportive family, and our conversations were always high on tactfulness. We made sure there was lots of kindness and empathy when we dealt with each other. However, we weren't as high on the truth side of things. It's not that we were dishonest, but we held back sharing things that may have been hard for the other person to hear, or would result in an uncomfortable conversation, because we didn't want to hurt one another's feelings or be disrespectful. Sadly, when I look back, I think we missed out on providing each other with the full value of our perspectives and pushback.

I have also worked with a lot of leaders who pride themselves on being "truth-tellers." They tell me that they "call it like they see it" and "say it like it is." Yet when I talk with members of these leaders' teams, it's clear they see things quite differently. They describe a team culture where everyone is "walking on eggshells," waiting for the next time they get called out in public, embarrassed, or caught up in another unhealthy conflict.

The teams that I've worked with and been a part of that have been the most effective were the ones with exceptional communication skills. Team members had the courage to be truthful and candid with one another, and they had the courage to own the impact of their words, embracing tactfulness and empathy as a result. They realized that in order to experience next-level teamwork, being truthful and being tactful is a package deal.

CHAPTER 5

ALIGNING TO WIN

Promoting Collaboration AND Independence

COLLABORATION — *Working together in such a way that each person contributes their strengths, expertise, and perspective. Leveraging diversity to gain innovative and effective results.*

INDEPENDENCE — *Team members take individual ownership of their tasks and responsibilities, managing their time effectively and making decisions autonomously.*

STEP 1: UNDERSTAND

To achieve next-level teamwork, it's crucial that your team members are skillfully aligned. This involves not only working collaboratively, but also having the ability to work independently when necessary.

As the following graphic illustrates, there are positive results that come exclusively from focusing on *both* collaboration *and* independence. At the same time, there are inevitable negative results if you overfocus on one side to the neglect of the other.

TENSION
Promoting Collaboration AND Independence

+

POSITIVE RESULTS OF
PROMOTING COLLABORATION

- Higher quality work through more ideas and feedback
- More energy, engagement, and fun
- Efficiency due to less back and forth

+

POSITIVE RESULTS OF
PROMOTING INDEPENDENCE

- Productivity increased by dividing and conquering
- People can focus on their roles and work more flexibly
- Skills and confidence are developed by "just doing it"

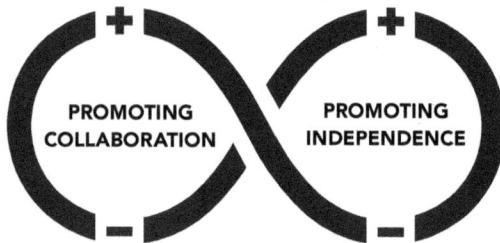

+

PROMOTING
COLLABORATION

PROMOTING
INDEPENDENCE

−

NEGATIVE RESULTS
WHEN **OVERDONE**

- People can't put their heads down and get things done
- Constantly coordinating details slows people down
- Creates unnecessary codependency

NEGATIVE RESULTS
WHEN **OVERDONE**

- Quality declines due to lack of perspective and feedback
- Work is less fun, and team relationships suffer
- Duplication and mistakes due to silos and blind spots

STEP 2: ASSESS

Reflect on how your team has been aligned this past season. Has your team been experiencing all the benefits that come from working collaboratively? Have you also been tapping into the positive results that come from working independently?

Take a look at the following chart and assess in which of the four quadrants your team is currently spending the most time.

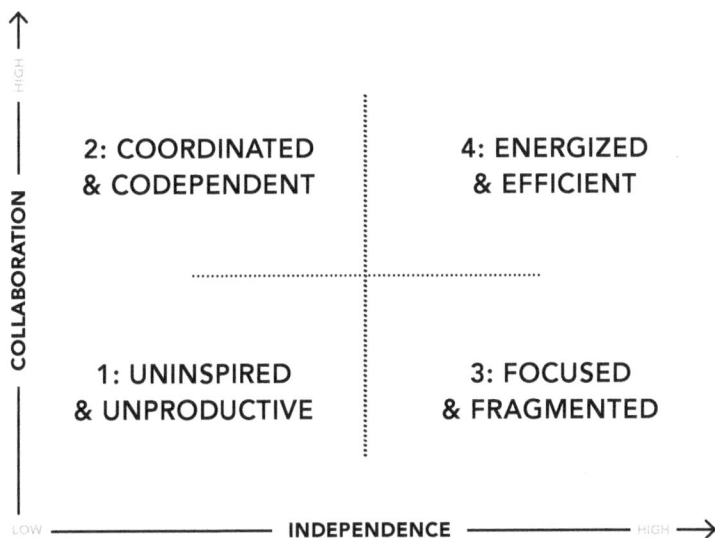

STEP 3: LEVERAGE

Regardless of which quadrant you are currently in, the goal is to spend as much time as possible in quadrant four. To do that, you have to start by being clear on these two things:

1. This is not a tension that will be managed well by chance; it will only be managed well by choice.

2. There isn't a one-size-fits-all formula or strategy that will work for every team. The level of collaborative work versus independent work your team needs to run effectively will be different from any other team's.

The good news is your team can develop a simple yet effective strategy to help you experience the positive results of working *both* collaboratively *and* independently, helping you to become more energized and efficient. The best way to do this is by identifying action steps and red flags.

Action Steps – These are one to three actions you (and/or your team) can take to gain or maintain the positive results of collaboration and one to three actions you can take to gain or maintain the positive results of independence. Your action steps must be measurable and objective (i.e., What are we committing to? Who is accountable? When will this happen?). To give you a picture of what an action step might look like, here are two that our team developed years ago, which we still use today:

> **Action Step for Collaboration:** *Calendar Commitment* – Our team made a weekly commitment to allocate three hours of time in our calendars for collaborative work. This didn't necessarily mean that we had to work collaboratively during that time, but rather it ensured that our teammates were available to provide assistance whenever we needed to tap into the power of collaboration on a project, proposal, or problem.

> The fascinating thing was that after implementing this strategy, healthy collaboration started occurring

much more frequently and in a more efficient and manageable manner. It's worth noting that during this three-hour block, individuals could still schedule calls or brief meetings, but they had to commit to keeping the majority of the block available for collaboration.

Action Step for Independence: *Passion Projects* – The team spent time looking at current things we were routinely collaborating on that we didn't necessarily need to be. Once we identified these things, we started to explore how to allow individuals who were the most skilled and/or passionate about those tasks/ projects to own them.

For instance, my colleague, Claudia, and I worked together on planning and writing for our marketing efforts (e.g., website, social media, etc.), but I realized that I was passionate about this work and thought about it all the time whereas it was more of a chore for her. Consequently, we agreed that I would take ownership of this work moving forward and only involve her when I needed her perspective or feedback.

Ultimately, this process helped us identify a long list of areas where collaboration wasn't essential.

Red Flags – These are one to three early warning signs that your team is either over-collaborating or working too independently. In order to be effective, your red flags must be measurable and objective (i.e., What is the early warning sign? Who is responsible to track it? What will we do if it happens?). To help you visualize what a red flag might look like, here are two our team developed that have proved to be incredibly helpful:

Red Flag for Overdone Collaboration: *Groundhog Day* – During our weekly calendar commitment, we established a rule that if we were about to collaborate on a task we had worked on together in the past, we would pause and ask ourselves, "Are we collaborating just for the sake of collaboration, or does this project or situation still require collaborative effort?" We discovered that, about half the time, we didn't need to work on the situation collaboratively and could divide and conquer instead. The other half of the time, we recognized that collaborative work was necessary for achieving the best results, and we continued to work together.

Red Flag for Overdone Independence: *The Blindside* – As someone who values constant improvement, I often make changes to my workshops and keynotes to stay relevant and keep things interesting. However, my team pointed out that these changes are not always decided on collaboratively, and it's distracting and confusing to find out about them in real time during programs with clients.

To address this issue, we made a commitment that during co-facilitated programs, if a team member notices new content on a slide or handout they were not aware of, or realizes that changes were made to the PowerPoint slideshow without their knowledge, we would discuss within the next working day if we were working too independently. This has caused me to slow down and collaborate more effectively around program improvements, ensuring that everyone is informed and on the same page.

ALIGNING TO WIN

To unlock next-level teamwork, it's crucial to understand, assess, and optimize the balance between collaborative and independent work. Regardless of people's individual preferences, and regardless of whether you're working together in the office or in a remote setting, team members need to be constantly committed to managing this tension in a healthy way.

This means your team members understand that, at times, the best way to move things forward and achieve optimal results is to empower each other with the freedom to get things done on their own. But on the other hand, everyone is equally committed to bringing people together—understanding that, at times, none of us is as smart as all of us.[1]

There is no single formula that can be applied to every team to make it successful. Each team is unique, and the approach that works best for one may not work for another. Some teams function like soccer or hockey teams where collaboration is key and tasks need to be passed back and forth constantly in order to progress. Others resemble a track-and-field relay team where individuals can work independently on their responsibilities as long as they effectively execute their handoff to other team members at the right time.[2]

Regardless of which type of team your workplace most closely resembles, it's important to strike a balance between collaboration and independence. When done correctly, this can help to create a dynamic environment where team members feel empowered and energized, leading to greater efficiency and productivity.

CHAPTER 6

THE OWNERSHIP PARADOX

Increasing Empowerment AND Accountability

EMPOWERMENT — *Having the autonomy to make decisions and take ownership of tasks. Being trusted by colleagues and leaders to independently contribute to the team's success.*

ACCOUNTABILITY — *Being responsible for meeting objectives and delivering quality work. Accepting feedback, learning from mistakes, and striving to constantly improve.*

STEP 1: UNDERSTAND

To create a fully engaged and ownership-driven team, members need to be empowered and trusted to solve problems on their own. However, to be effective, this team culture of empowerment needs to be balanced with a healthy level of accountability.

This graphic explains the positive outcomes that can only be achieved by focusing on *both* empowerment *and* accountability. It also demonstrates how focusing excessively on one side while neglecting the other will inevitably lead to negative consequences.

TENSION
Increasing Empowerment AND Accountability

POSITIVE RESULTS OF
INCREASING EMPOWERMENT

- People are motivated and engaged
- Taps into unique and creative ways to get work done
- Increases learning and problem solving

POSITIVE RESULTS OF
INCREASING ACCOUNTABILITY

- People are deliberate and mindful when taking action
- Team members follow through on commitments
- Healthy boundaries on team members' authority

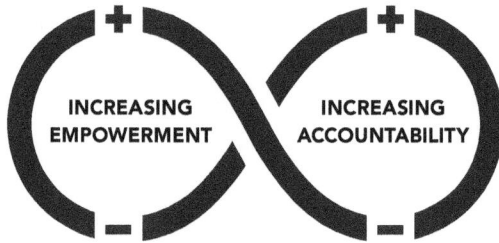

INCREASING EMPOWERMENT   **INCREASING ACCOUNTABILITY**

NEGATIVE RESULTS
WHEN **OVERDONE**

- Poor decisions are made due to lack of experience
- Quality goes down and balls are dropped
- People go beyond the limits of their authority

NEGATIVE RESULTS
WHEN **OVERDONE**

- People are frustrated by micromanagement
- Creativity and ownership are stifled
- People lack the authority to solve problems on their own

STEP 2: ASSESS

Take a moment to reflect on your team's meetings and inter-actions over the past season. Did your team experience all the benefits that come from a high level of empowerment? Did you also have the necessary level of accountability to be effective?

Take a look at the following chart and assess in which of the four quadrants your team is currently spending the most time.

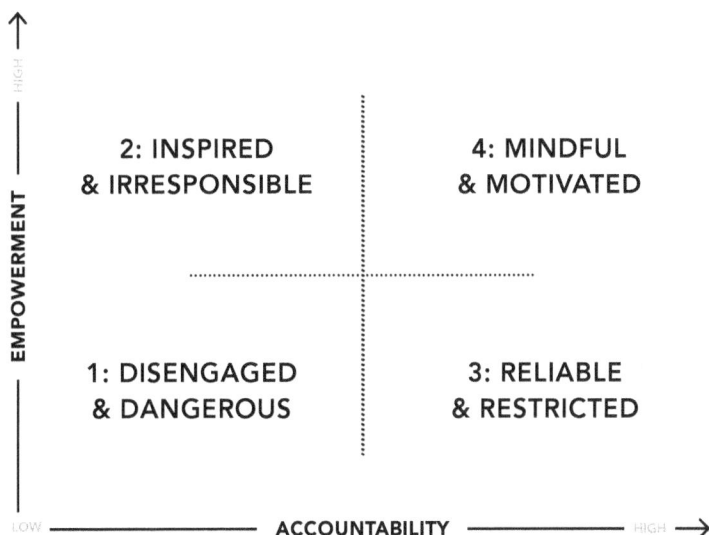

2: INSPIRED & IRRESPONSIBLE	**4: MINDFUL & MOTIVATED**
1: DISENGAGED & DANGEROUS	**3: RELIABLE & RESTRICTED**

EMPOWERMENT (HIGH ↑)

ACCOUNTABILITY (LOW — HIGH →)

STEP 3: LEVERAGE

No matter which quadrant your team is currently spending the most time in, your goal is to strive for quadrant four. The good news is that there are practical actions you can take to get there. It is possible to experience the positive outcomes of *both* empow-erment *and* accountability, resulting in a more mindful and motivated team.

INCREASING EMPOWERMENT

"Control leads to compliance; autonomy leads to engagement."

– DANIEL H. PINK

NEW YORK TIMES *BESTSELLING AUTHOR*

Accommodate Learning Styles – If you're going to increase empowerment, you must be both deliberate in and skilled at teaching people to do things on their own. What makes this tricky is that people have diverse learning styles. I have found through research[1] and experience that people's learning styles can best be defined in one of three ways:

1. **Experimenters** – These are people who learn best by "just doing it." They need to be given the ability to try things out and learn through action.

2. **Imitators** – These are people who learn best by seeing it done well and then replicating it. They gain confidence from coming alongside someone who is skilled and experienced.

3. **Analyzers** – These are people who read the instruction manuals for their TVs and appliances. They love information and need to know all the facts and details in order to be confident.

As a leader, if you take a one-size-fits-all approach to teaching and training (i.e., mimicking your own personal learning style), you'll probably only succeed about one-third of the time. For example, the worst thing you can do to an experimenter is overwhelm them with too much information upfront. The quickest way to shut down an imitator is to ask them to try something without seeing it done well a few times first. And if you fail to give an analyzer the information they need, they'll be resentful and lack the confidence needed for success.

When it comes to providing the teaching and training required to effectively empower someone, you need to go beyond the golden rule of treating people the way you want to be treated, and instead, treat people the way *they* want to be treated. Find out their individual learning style and then train them in a way that accommodates it.

If you're not sure what someone's learning style is, you can always gain clarity by having them answer these questions:[2]

- When in your career do you think you were learning the most?

- Why did you learn so much?

- What's the best way for me to help you learn?

Define Boundaries – When you empower others, you give them more freedom to make decisions and take ownership of tasks. However, it's important to be clear about the limits of this empowerment. For example, when it comes to spending money, make sure everyone knows how much they can spend before needing approval.

Similarly, when dealing with customer requests or complaints, establish guidelines for when changes can be made independently and when collaboration is necessary. It's also important to remember that these boundaries may need to be adjusted over time, so ongoing communication is essential to ensuring success as you increase empowerment.

INCREASING ACCOUNTABILITY

"Being held accountable is an act of generosity and compassion. It is a gift that someone gives us to correct our wrongs, unlearn, and do better for the sake of our own growth. It might be uncomfortable, but it is worth the discomfort."

– MINAA B.

AUTHOR AND MENTAL HEALTH EDUCATOR

Step Up Support – There's a funny saying that dog trainers use to teach dog owners what to do if their puppy has an accident in the house during the weeks of potty training:

1. Grab a newspaper,

2. Roll it up, and

3. Hit *yourself* on the head.

The idea is that it's not the dog's fault! You should have been more involved and supported the puppy better.

Similarly, as you give your team members more freedom, they will need higher levels of support than ever before. Accountability isn't just holding people responsible and assigning blame. It's ongoing performance management, coaching, debriefing, and celebrating successes. This takes time!

In the short term, it will always be easier to do things on your own. And there will also be a learning curve during which you should expect mistakes (i.e., learning opportunities). But in the long term, by stepping up the level of accountability and support you provide, you'll increase both efficiency and productivity.

Training vs. Micromanaging – When you provide accountability and check in on the people you are empowering, one of the biggest criticisms you may face is that you're micromanaging them. While it's important to listen to this feedback and remember that your way is not always the *only* way, it's also important to recognize the difference between micromanaging and training.

Training involves providing the necessary instruction and supervision for people to do things correctly, thereby aligning with your corporate culture and ensuring the level of quality and service your customers expect and deserve.

In his book *EntreLeadership*,[3] author Dave Ramsey does a great job of delineating between training and micromanaging. When hearing him speak about this topic, I wrote down some of his words of wisdom that I think sum up this difference perfectly: "When someone doesn't know how to do the thing the way you want it done, it is not micromanaging to correct them, and teach them, and mentor them. It's called training. To let them continue to do it the wrong way is stupid."

THE OWNERSHIP PARADOX

The concept of ownership in an organization is an interesting one. I can't even begin to count the number of leaders who have reached out to me asking if I could help instill a "culture of ownership" in their organization. They want people to be more responsible and default to going above and beyond when it comes to their job.

I get it! As a business owner myself, I know that for the company to truly thrive, my team needs to work with a high level of ownership. But here's the thing—they don't own the company. Only I do. And as much as I try to create a great work environment and remain competitive in my compensation strategy, only I get to enjoy many of the perks of ownership.

So how do you instill the value of ownership in people who aren't actually owners? I think the best answer to this question comes from author and thought-leader Daniel Pink. In his book, *Drive: The Surprising Truth About What Motivates Us*,[4] he draws on four decades of research on human motivation to conclude that true ownership comes from a blend of:

A. Autonomy,

B. Mastery, and

C. Purpose.

If you delve into his work (and I strongly recommend that you do), it affirms this need to embrace *both* empowerment *and* accountability. It may seem obvious that his value of autonomy can only happen when leaders are willing to empower their employees, but his other two values—mastery and purpose—will not come from empowerment alone. They will only exist when leaders can provide healthy levels of accountability—the kind of accountability that equips, envisions, and supports what is necessary for empowered employees to thrive.

In short, empowerment and accountability only work when they are working together, and finding healthy tension between them is critical if you want to experience next-level teamwork in your organization.

CHAPTER 7

DON'T SETTLE FOR DYSFUNCTION

It's Time to Start Looking Forward to Monday Mornings

MOST TEAMS DON'T WORK

I kicked off this book with some disheartening statistics: Nearly 75% of professionals find themselves in dysfunctional teams.[1] Moreover, based on their negative team experiences, only 24% of professionals would willingly choose to work in teams if given the option.[2]

The unfortunate reality is that most teams simply don't work!

A primary cause for this dysfunction comes from people's inability to understand, assess, and leverage the five unavoidable tensions discussed in this book. In a world that mistakenly perceives tension as inherently negative, most teams choose to either ignore or avoid it.

Drawing from my experience working with hundreds of organizations and thousands of teams worldwide, I have witnessed three inevitable outcomes when teams fail to embrace tension and navigate it in a constructive manner:

1. The Perpetual Pendulum – In this phenomenon, teams continuously swing back and forth between two extremes, driven by short-term and simplistic strategies. Initially, teams wholeheartedly embrace one side of a tension, such as empowerment, and proclaim it as the key focus (e.g., "This is the year of empowerment!"). However, as they excessively prioritize one value at the expense of the other, negative consequences inevitably emerge (e.g., "Uh-oh, people are making mistakes and working outside their areas of expertise!").

In response to the unfavourable outcomes, teams mistakenly assume that the value they are prioritizing must be incorrect, leading them to swing to the other side for a while (e.g., "Okay, now we realize that moving forward, it's all about accountability!"). Unfortunately, this swing is short-lived as it becomes evident that the new approach also falls short, prompting a swing back to the initial position. This perpetual back-and-forth exhausts team members, erodes their trust in leadership's direction, and ultimately diminishes engagement.

2. The Not-So-Great Divide – Due to an inability to embrace complexity, teams find themselves trapped in the confines of a limited mindset—seeing things as strictly right or wrong, good or bad, for or against. This narrow perspective leads to a dangerous divide among team members and results in relational polarization. It's a tale of "You're either with us or against us."

Sadly, this division creates echo chambers within the team where individuals surround themselves with only like-minded colleagues who affirm their views. Staying quiet during the meeting, they speak freely in the "meeting" after the meeting where they reinforce their views with people on their side. In doing so, they unknowingly shut out the potential for healthy and creative tension that could arise from engaging with team members holding different perspectives. As a result, they operate with significant blind spots and limited thinking, and the level of trust and psychological safety within the team remains low.

3. The Mediocrity Trap – The wasted energy and productivity tied to the perpetual pendulum combined with the lack of collaboration and synergy linked to the not-so-great divide result in a team that is stuck in survival mode. Meetings become mere formalities and lack the critical pushback and healthy opposition that drives meaningful dialogue. As a result, the essential ingredients for making ground-breaking decisions and taking innovative approaches are nowhere to be found.

As lazy thinking takes hold and relational cliques form, high-performing and high-potential team members begin seeking better opportunities elsewhere. Meanwhile, average performers settle into comfortable complacency. Before you know it, the team is trapped in a culture of mediocrity, trudging through each week with the sole aim of making it to Friday.

SOME TEAMS DO WORK!

The great news is that some teams choose a road less travelled, and rather than ignoring or avoiding key tensions, they lean into them and learn how to leverage them. And this truly does make *all* the difference.

Time and time again, I have seen three predictable outcomes that teams experience when they have the skills and courage needed to tap into the power of healthy tension:

1. From "Right" to "Best" – When teams transcend overly simplistic Either/Or thinking, which demands a binary right-or-wrong approach, and embrace Both/And thinking, which acknowledges the validity of multiple perspectives, they develop a vibrant and dynamic culture. As a result, team members no longer squander their time and damage their relationships through endless debates over what is the "right" answer.

Instead, they channel their efforts into collaborative discussions aimed at identifying the "best" answer from a variety of solid options. Furthermore, they recognize that this option may not remain the best option in the future, thereby fostering a constant readiness for change and a receptive attitude toward innovation.

2. From Discord to Harmony – A remarkable transformation occurs when teams begin to embrace healthy tension—they realize that there's wisdom in resistance. They start to understand that they don't have to *exchange* their values and viewpoints in order to *expand* them. This shift leads team members to actively seek out diverse perspectives and constructive pushback from others.

Consequently, meetings become lively and open with individuals expressing their views while attentively listening to others. Ultimately, this creates a culture of openness and candour where people feel safe and trust levels soar.

3. From Surviving to Thriving – In the book, *Built to Last: Successful Habits of Visionary Companies*,[3] authors Jim Collins and Jerry Porras dig into the secrets behind organizations that consistently achieve exceptional performance and influence over extended periods of time. These companies don't just have temporary success; they routinely outperform their competitors for decades.

Collins and his team conducted an in-depth investigation to uncover the factors that set these organizations apart. They discovered that these companies were able to harness the power of healthy tension, using what Collins refers to as the Genius of the AND:

Instead of being oppressed by the "Tyranny of the OR," highly visionary companies liberate themselves with the "Genius of the AND"—the ability to embrace both extremes of a number of dimensions at the same time. Instead of choosing between A OR B, they figure out a way to have both A AND B.

Teams and organizations that choose to leverage the key tensions discussed in this book can tap into a true competitive advantage and move from surviving to thriving.

WHY THIS MATTERS

In Chapter 1, I introduced you to Matt and Priya. To refresh your memory, Matt was the one who dreaded Monday mornings and whose team experience was a negative one. I wish I could tell you that the character of Matt is purely a fictional one, but sadly, it is based on one of my closest friends—a person who always brought 110% to his job, was passionate about making a difference, and prided himself on being a team player.

Recently, after Matt took what seemed like a dream job, he quickly realized he'd walked into a toxic team culture. I witnessed his journey from optimism—believing that he had the ability to make positive change in the team—to frustration—realizing his impact was limited—and finally to defeat and apathy. At this point, he was even starting to question his entire profession, which he had excelled at and previously loved.

What was particularly difficult to witness was how this negative team experience affected Matt outside of work. He became less happy and enjoyable to be around. Even his family noticed the change and constantly asked him what was wrong. Matt's negative team experience was taking a toll on his overall life.

IT'S NOT OKAY!

Every Monday morning, our team at Leaders for Leaders gathers for a quick huddle. Before discussing the workshops and keynotes we'll be delivering in the week ahead, we always revisit our mission statement. What makes our mission statement somewhat unique is that it doesn't just outline the goals we aim to achieve; it also explains the underlying reason, the "why" behind our "what."

The concluding sentence of our mission is: "We must accomplish these goals because too many people have to deal with toxic, underperforming workplaces." Every week we remind ourselves that there are countless individuals like Matt out there, and quite simply, that's not okay!

What gives me hope is that every week, I get to work with clients who prove to me that some teams actually do work. They serve as a reminder that amidst the Matts in the world, there are also individuals like Priya who genuinely look forward to Monday mornings. These individuals are not part of perfect teams (because let's face it, perfect teams don't exist), but they belong to teams that are healthy, high performing, and committed to getting better.

And what's incredible is that I get to see firsthand how these team members evolve into better versions of themselves—both at work and at home—through the support and constructive feedback they receive from their peers. Their positive team experience is a catalyst for them living full and vibrant lives.

I can't provide you with a simple formula or quick-fix solution to make your team work. There are no easy answers or miracle cures. However, what this playbook offers is a winning strategy. By implementing the "plays" outlined in this book and being dedicated to understanding, assessing, and leveraging the five tensions, you will set your team on the path to success. Through this approach, you will unlock the potential for next-level teamwork.

You spend most of your waking hours Monday to Friday working within a team. Make sure those are hours you look forward to each week. Life is simply too short to settle for working in a dysfunctional team!

FREE RESOURCE

To thank you for purchasing this playbook, I want to provide you with a free resource that will allow you to create a personal action plan around key concepts and big ideas.

Simply visit www.timarnold.ca/teams to download the Personal Action Plan. This digital journal includes chapter summaries, tension maps, and assessment grids as well as space for you to create a plan you can immediately put into action.

WWW.TIMARNOLD.CA/TEAMS

NEXT STEPS

Check out these enjoyable and effective ways to help your entire organization tap into next-level teamwork:

Keynotes – One-hour presentations that motivate and inspire your audience to reach higher and dig deeper. Virtual and in-person options available.

Workshops – Insightful and engaging virtual and in-person programs that boost morale, develop leadership, and align teams to thrive.

Online Course – A self-directed, five-module course that will help you thrive in a world of complexity and polarization. Includes teaching videos, an editable workbook, and reflection activities.

SIMPLY VISIT WWW.TIMARNOLD.CA TO LEARN MORE.

REFERENCES

CHAPTER 1

1. Behnam Tabrizi, "75% of Cross-Functional Teams Are Dysfunctional," *Harvard Business Review*, June 23, 2015.

2. University of Phoenix, "University of Phoenix Survey Reveals Nearly Seven-in-Ten Workers Have Been Part of Dysfunctional Teams," *PRNewswire*, January 2013.

CHAPTER 2

1. Marcus Buckingham, Curt Coffman, *First, Break All the Rules: What the World's Greatest Managers Do Differently*, Simon & Schuster, 1999.

2. Gallup Inc., State of the Global Workplace, Gallup Press, 2017.

3. Patrick Lencioni, *The Five Dysfunctions of a Team*, Jossey-Bass, 2002.

4. Stephen Covey, *The 7 Habits of Highly Effective People: Restoring the Character Ethic*, Simon & Schuster, 1989.

CHAPTER 3

1. Marcus Buckingham, "What Great Managers Do," *Harvard Business Review*, March 2005.

2. Amy C. Edmondson, *The Fearless Organization: Creating Psychological Safety in the Workplace for Learning, Innovation, and Growth*, John Wiley & Sons, 2018.

CHAPTER 4

1. Joe Griffin, "7-11 Breathing," Human Givens Institute, accessed March 28, 2023, https://www.hgi.org.uk/resources/delve-our-extensive-library/resources-and-techniques/7-11-breathing-how-does-deep

2. Susan David, Twitter.com, January 14, 2021, accessed June 4, 2023, https://twitter.com/SusanDavid_PhD/status/1349747542209286144

CHAPTER 5

1. Ken Blanchard, "None of Us Is as Smart as All of Us," Kenblanchardbooks.com, May 25, 2022, accessed June 4, 2023, https://www.kenblanchardbooks.com/no-one-of-us-is-as-smart-as-all-of-us/

2. Salesforce.org, "Adam Grant's 6 Tips for Building More Engaged Marketing Teams," Salesforce, December 16, 2021, accessed June 4, 2023, https://www.salesforce.org/blog/adam-grant-engaged-marketing-teams/

CHAPTER 6

1. Hugh Phillips, *The Effective Trainer: A Practical Guide to Training and Development*, Kogan Page, 2015.

2. Marcus Buckingham, Curt Coffman, *First, Break All the Rules: What the World's Greatest Managers Do Differently*, Simon & Schuster, 1999.

3. Dave Ramsey, *EntreLeadership: 20 Years of Practical Business Wisdom from the Trenches*, Howard Books, 2011.

4. Daniel Pink, *Drive: The Surprising Truth About What Motivates Us*, Riverhead Books, 2009.

CHAPTER 7

1. Behnam Tabrizi, "75% of Cross-Functional Teams Are Dysfunctional," Harvard Business Review, June 23, 2015.

2. University of Phoenix, "University of Phoenix Survey Reveals Nearly Seven-in-Ten Workers Have Been Part of Dysfunctional Teams," *PRNewswire*, January 2013.

3. Jim Collins, Jerry Porras, *Built to Last: Successful Habits of Visionary Companies*, HarperBusiness, 2002.

ABOUT THE AUTHOR

Tim Arnold has spent over two decades helping leaders manage complexity, increase resilience, and deliver results within organizations such as the United Nations, Compassion International, Royal Bank of Canada, Allstate Insurance, Toyota, and Siemens.

After running both a for-profit business and a homeless shelter, Tim leverages his real-world experience to help organizations pursue both profit and purpose. His work focuses on helping leaders unleash the superpower of Both/And thinking in an Either/Or world.

Beyond leadership and team development, Tim is an avid fisherman, world traveller, and really bad hockey player. His biggest accomplishments are being dad to Declan and Avryl and husband to Becky.

WWW.TIMARNOLD.CA

WWW.LEADERSFORLEADERS.CA